BOOKS BY THE AUTHOR

Forever Free

This title is available as a free eBook at
WiseWordWind.com.

Falling Into All
Prayer Sayer Song
Rise Eyes Wise

Forever Free

BEN R. TEETER

WISE
WORD
WIND
PRESS

Wise Word Wind Press
P.O Box 371732
San Diego, CA 92137
WiseWordWind.com

This is not a work of fiction. Names, characters, places, locations and incidents are all real and are meant to bear a relationship to real-life individuals, living and dead, and actual places, business establishments, locations, events and incidents. Any resemblance to the reader and to those he or she may know is entirely intentional.

Cover Design by Randy Gibbs

Book Layout by Golden Ratio Book Design

First Edition

Printed in the United States of America

ISBN: 978-1-7349891-3-7 (Trade paperback)
ISBN: 978-1-7349891-2-0 (Ebook)

Library of Congress Control Number: 2021913422

Forever Free

Sky

Falls
Through,

Body
Erased.

Where
I
Was,

Graced.

You
Give
Me

The
Glittering
Pour

Of
Your

Prosperous
Infinity.

You
Give
Me

The
Beautiful
Nothing

Of
The
Free.

Where

Silence
Is
Being
Heard,

Loved,

It
Rushes
In,

Touches,

Engages
In

The
Impossible
Friendship.

The
Thank
You

Grows,

Crescendos,

Bursts,

Goes.

Then
Goes
The
Me.

And
Then

The
You

Goes,

Too.

Full
Eye

Of

Soul's
Skin

Feels
Ony

Heaven's
Aware
Still
Wind.

Stumbling,

The
Moth
Came,

Entered,

Became

Only

Naked
Flame.

No
Matter

Under

How
Much

The
Infinite

Poverty

I

Pouring
Bucket

Try
To
Create,

Of
Your
All.

I
Fail
At
It

The
Time

We
Feel,

So
Flowing
Like
A
River,

Could
Encounter,

Might
It
Not?

A
Waterfall,
Majestic,

Rainbowed,
White,
Tall,

A
Sudden
Roaring

Into
All.

Skilled
Ignorers

That
We
Are,

We
Focus
Into

Pittances
Of
Worry,

While
Our
Lives

Are
Clothed

In
Infinite
Cascading
Draperies,

Life's
Unbounded
Beauties,

Housed
In
The
Exalted

Infinite
Hall

Whose
Hand
Holds

Of
All.

The Day
And
The Night,

Fed
By
The
Hand

Of
The
One

The
Day
Is
Filled.
So,

With
His
Care,

There
Is
No
Room

For
More
New
Prayer.

For
He
Is
So
Close,

Already
All,

There
Is
No
Space

To
Reach
Or
Call.

Some
Times
It's
Nice

An

Empty
Funnel

To
Let
A
Busy
Mind

From
Heart

Up
Straight,

Lie
Down
And
Die,

To
Empty
Sky,

And
Place

And
Wait.

Peace
Pours
In

Upon

My
Crumbling
Questions.

The
Sky
Has
Descended,

No
Need
Now

Filling
The
Stones
And
Rivers

To
Fly
Up.

And
All
The

Up
Is
Now

Things
And
Creatures.

Completely
Among
Us.

The
Shadow

Proves

The
Sun.

Puppet
Mortal
Man

Dances
Upon
Strings

Of

Infinite
Things.

Sit.

Open.

Release
Soul's
Skin.

Let
All

In.

Man
Mind
Goes
Searching

With
A
Cutting
Tool,

For
Darkness
With
A
Light,

For
The
Certain

For
Silence
With
A
Name,

With
A
Question,

For
Fullness
With
A
Need.

For
All,

O,

How
Shall
He
Succeed?

Can
You

Point,
Or
Place
Finger,

Linger
Any
Where,

On
Any
Particle,

In
Any
Article,

Where
Cannot
Be
Found

Infinitude
Profound?

Miraculous.

The
Infinite
World

Disappears
Or
Reassembles

With
The
Winking,

Twinkling
Of
My

I.

Here
Is

The
Universe

That
I
Wear.

A
Man

Sits
There.

The
Infiniteness

Here
Fills,

Leaves
Me

No
Room

For

Mere
Plenty.

Enemies
Arise
In
Mirrors.

O
Man,

Let
The
Infinity

Before
Your
Gaze

Amaze.

Can
A
Worm

Have
Wings?

O
My!

Ask
Any

Butterfly.

26

No
Need,

Ever-
More,

To
Fly,

When

One
Is

Already

Sky.

Let
This

Atom
Spin.

I
Am
The

Still
Point

Within.

The

All
That
Is

Is
Being

What
Is
Here.

Infinity
Is
Me.

No
Skin
In

This
Eternity,

Except

What Errored
Man

May
See.

A
Wobbling
Axis

Comes
To
Poise.

There
Is
Music

Where
Was
Noise.

This
Man,

He
Was
Forsaken.

I
Have
Shaken,

To
Awaken,

Though
He,

At
Times,

Thought
It
Meant

Lo,

Limitations
Lie.

All
Is
I.

The
Personal

Withdraws
Into

The
Perfections,

Stationed
Around

The
Still.

Fragments
Rejoin,

And
Never
Were

Asunder.

What
A
Wonder!

As
The
Man
Atom

Clear
Sphere

Vibrates

Around
Dot,

Around
Its
Self
Spot,

Infinite,

Is
Begot.

A
Universe,

Light
And
Sound,

Now

Is

One
And
Same,

The
First
Burst

Different
Only

That
Came.

In
Man's
Name:

Encountering
Someone

Of
A
Different

Pace
Or
Mind,

Best
Practice
Is,

Be
Kind.

This,

That
I
Cannot
Seize,

Sees.

Suddenly,

'Nothing'
Happens,

    The
    Pristine.

And

Is

Seen.

And

All
That
Is

Is
Held
In

Emptiness,

My
Long
Lost
Friend,

Here
You
Are,

At
Last,

Again.

The
Body
Mind,

We
Find,

Would

Toss
The
Fruit,

And

Keep
The
Rind.

All
Things
Lie

Within
The

Twinkling

Of
An

I.

Into
Existence

I
Whistle
A
World

Around
A
Man.

I
Step

Outside
Of
The
All,

Clear,

And
Find
My
Self

Already
Here.

Perfection

Dots
The
Landscape

With

Versions
Of
Itself.

O
Celestial,

Temporary
Things.

Of

Infinite
Wings,

Abide
For
A
Moment

In
These,

The
Seemingly

The
Nameless

Arrives

Among

The
Names.

Perfection

Is
In
The

I

Of
The

Be

Holder.

This.

Is

A
Good
Time

For

The
Perfect
Moment.

ABOUT THE AUTHOR

 Who is the Author?

This question is best answered by looking into the author's finished pages, which stand ready for the reading.

But, in the interests of social convention, here is some biographical data to clothe this character.

The early years of the author were steeped in several cultures.

The author as a youngster spent long hours and years in the laconic hard scrabble labor of rural Appalachian mountain life, his father's roots.

The author's mother came from the prosperous rolling and flat farmlands of rural Maryland, close-knit family people of an old Pennsylvania Dutch background, who sang sweet acapela harmonies, while praying and working together.

The author grew up in both influences, while living in the midst of the robust cultural mix of the Washington D.C. environs.

The author left high school blessed with a scholarship to an exceptionally fine university, where he spent his four years, wandering somewhat, among the peaks of Man's intellectual achievement.

The Writing Seminars were among the most memorable experiences of the time there, hours of sharing words among fellow poets, lounging around a large and darkly aged conference table.

In the cultural uproar of the 1968-69 senior year, studies were eclipsed, as the author's interests exploded into off-campus venues and activities, not in the political actions of the day, but in the spiritual, metaphysical and transcendental.

In this vibrant time, the City of Baltimore burgeoned with opportunities for close friendships, learning and practice with various yogis from India, gypsies, highly conscious artists and mystics of various kinds, along with a matured Theosophical Lodge and Rosicrucian Lodge, AMORC, all of this guided by the posters and amazingly well-stocked shelves of the New Age Bookstore, where meditators gathered, crowded together seated on the floor on Tuesday evenings. The author was a part of spiritual communes that started up and renovated spaces in which to work and live together.

This storm of Baltimore life came on, seemed to last forever, and then passed suddenly, with an abrupt departure to a small place in Vermont's north woods.

Then stretched decades of living various places, supported by working with hands and small building business activity, with years of life's lessons in family living with children, years of a spiritual-martial practice, years spent close with a guru from India, and years of working with a spiritually oriented mind training course.

In recent years, the art of word-craft, practiced since childhood, came to the fore.

A body of privately written work slowly accumulated, waiting for the writer to feel ready for its release.

FROM THE PUBLISHER

Hello Dear Reader!

We hope that you are enjoying *Forever Free* as much as we enjoyed producing it and putting it out into the world.

We also hope that you feel it worthwhile to help spread the word about this book in your community of like-minded readers.

Your review on Amazon will go a long way toward letting other people know about *Forever Free*.

If you would like to help out (every little bit helps), will you please post a review on Amazon, or where you purchased a copy?

Do you know someone who would enjoy reading *Forever Free?* Download a free copy on our website, at WiseWordWind.com

Plus, we offer weekly fresh words from Ben by email and on social media. Be sure to subscribe and join our audience of loyal readers. Visit WiseWordWind.com to sign up.

If you want to connect with Ben directly, email him at Ben@WiseWordWind.com.

Thank you!

-The Team at Wise Word Wind Press

Printed in Great Britain
by Amazon

21751405R00038